W[illegible]D FOR LOVE

Understanding Attachment Theory & Deepening connections

NATASHA ARRINDELL

LIFE AND SUCCESS PUBLISHING
www.abookinsideyou.com

For permission requests, write to the publisher, addressed
"Attention: Permissions Coordinator" at the email address below:
Life and Success Media Ltd
e-mail: info@abookinsideyou.com
www.abookinsideyou.com

WIRED FOR BONDING
Understanding Attachment Theory
& Deepening Connections

ISBN: 978-1-7384586-0-8
Cover Design: **MIA**Design.com

CONTENTS

CONTENTS

DEDICATION

First and foremost, all praise and thanks to God Almighty for the blessings of Grace, Mercy, and Love in my life. I am humbled and grateful to know You.

To my beloved children, Shadrach, Soraya, and Abigail - you are my greatest teachers and inspirations. I am honoured to be your mother and cherish our lifelong bond.

To my steadfast friend Karin Bultje, thank you for your faithful support, feedback, and encouragement at every step of my journey to Secure Attachment and in writing this book.

To Peter Phelps, for our insightful talks and your guidance as a therapist and friend. You've helped me grow.

To my 'adopted' mum Miss June, for surrounding me with the motherly love I longed for. You embraced me fully.

To Kelley W, for standing by me unconditionally, even when it is challenging. Your loyalty uplifts me.

To Jacqueline Francis, for continually nudging me forward in bringing this book to life. I appreciate your enthusiasm.

To Allan Sealy, for your empathy, care, and patience as I progressed in security. You embody compassion.

To Ruth C., I have anchored your wise words in my heart: “Trust in trust.” That is the key to changing from insecure to secure attachment. Thank you, beautiful soul.

To my colleagues, Joel Dawes, Casey Howard, and Jermaine Lazarus - your admirable work protecting children inspires me daily.

And finally, to all my loved ones - family, friends, mentors. Your support through this journey is woven into every page. My deep and endless thanks.

FOREWORD

As a mother, my deepest wish was for my three children to grow up feeling secure and confident in themselves and their relationships. I intuitively felt that providing consistent love, support, and emotional attunement from the start could help foster strong attachment bonds that would serve them well throughout life. The research now clearly validates that early secure attachments create a foundation for thriving.

My own life experience reflected more of a challenge. Though I strived to be present and available, my tendency towards Avoidant Attachment stemming from childhood led me to struggle with emotional distancing. Through my parenting journey, I became determined to change my ingrained patterns. I owe it to my children to model healthy relationships.

This set me on a path of learning everything I could about Attachment Theory. The volumes of research on those early bonds shaping our self-concept, emotional regulation, and adult relationships resonated deeply. I recognized my avoidant tendencies but also grew convinced that with effort, developing earned security was possible. My personal quest inspired a calling to help others on their journey to security.

It is my hope this book provides understanding and inspiration to all readers, no matter where you are starting from. For those with insecure attachment, take heart that positive change, while difficult, is achievable. There are so many resources and strategies now to help rewrite old dynamics. For the securely attached, may you grow in compassion and skills to support loved ones struggling with anxiety, avoidance or instability in relationships. We all deserve to feel connected.

This book is written in the spirit of growth, healing, and actualization of healthier attachments. May we form, in the words of Sue Johnson, "Lasting ties that bind adults to one another and to their own deepest selves." Our collective well-being depends on it.

INTRODUCTION

Attachment theory has become a powerful tool for understanding how humans grow and form close bonds with others. This theory, first introduced by British psychologist John Bowlby in the 1950s, explores how the connections we make as children with our main caregivers shape our relationships and emotions as we grow into adults.

Bowlby believed that from the moment we're born, we have a natural tendency to form strong emotional connections with the individuals who take care of us, usually our parents. These special connections, called attachment bonds, play a huge role in helping us learn to handle our feelings and build healthy relationships. Mary Ainsworth, an American psychologist, added to this idea with her famous 1970 "Strange Situation" study. She found that different babies had different ways of attaching to their caregivers. Some felt secure, others were anxious, and some seemed distant. These patterns in babies' behaviours helped her create categories we now call attachment styles.

Later on, researchers Main and Solomon found a fourth style called "disorganized attachment." This happened when children didn't have a consistent way of connecting with their caregivers, often because of tough experiences like being neglected or abused.

Research over many years shows that these attachment styles we develop as babies can stick with us as we grow up. They shape how we act in our romantic relationships, friendships, work connections, and with our family. The way we are attached as children influences how we see ourselves, how we understand the world, how we deal with our feelings, and how we act in relationships. It's even linked to our mental well-being. While attachment theory helps explain a lot, it can't cover every detail or account for every difference across cultures. Still, it's had a big impact on areas like psychology and therapy.

This book is like a map that shows the journey of attachment theory. It talks about where it came from, the studies done, how it affects us as we grow, how it gets passed down through generations, and how we can make our connections stronger. New research shows that our attachment styles don't have to stay the same forever. With the right support and a desire to change, we can become more secure in how we connect with others. By understanding where our connections come from and being aware of them, we can heal from past hurts and build stronger, healthier relationships in the future.

1

Unraveling the Beginnings of Attachment Theory

In the ever-evolving landscape of psychology, attachment theory stands as a crucial framework that helps us make sense of how humans grow and connect. This transformative theory, which took shape in the mid-20th century, owes its foundation to the groundbreaking work of two brilliant minds: John Bowlby and Mary Ainsworth. Their tireless efforts, spanning the 1950s to the 1970s, have forever altered the way we perceive the early stages of emotional development.

Imagine stepping back in time to an era of immense psychological discovery. Here, John Bowlby emerged as a trailblazing thinker, guided by unconventional insights that challenged prevailing beliefs. He stepped away from the popular psychoanalytic and learning theories of his time and embraced the principles of ethology, a science that explores how evolution shapes behaviour. Bowlby's revolutionary idea centred on the innate instinct of infants to seek a strong attachment to their primary caregivers as a way to ensure survival.

This departure from conventional wisdom opened up new avenues of exploration into the complex world of human attachment.

At the heart of Bowlby's theory was the realization that our early experiences of emotional closeness and safety leave an indelible mark on our future relationships. This perspective stemmed from his understanding of attachment bonds as a biological need, woven into our very DNA through the course of evolution. Bowlby's pioneering insight marked a significant departure from the prevailing ideologies of his time and illuminated the profound role of attachment in human development.

Bowlby's groundbreaking work found a partner in Mary Ainsworth, a meticulous researcher who played a pivotal role in expanding and validating attachment theory. Her contributions came to fruition through the creation of the iconic "Strange Situation" procedure in 1970. This ingenious method involved observing infants as they experienced brief separations and reunions with their caregivers. The revelations were astonishing, revealing distinct behavior patterns in infants. Ainsworth identified three primary attachment styles: secure, anxious, and avoidant. This classification system marked a turning point, offering a comprehensive framework to understand the diverse ways in which attachment security unfolds. This framework laid the groundwork for a lifetime of exploration into the dynamics of attachment.

Ainsworth's work gave us a powerful lens through which we can understand the lasting impact of early relationships. Securely attached infants, who experienced consistent caregiving, tend to grow into adults who trust and value emotional intimacy. Anxious attachment, born from inconsistent care, can lead to adult relationships characterized by fear of abandonment. Avoidant attachment, often rooted in neglect, may lead to self-reliance and difficulty expressing emotions. These patterns, as Ainsworth illuminated, have far-reaching implications, shaping our perceptions of ourselves and our expectations of others in the complex tapestry of human relationships.

Building upon this foundation, subsequent researchers, including Main and Solomon, added another layer to attachment theory: the concept of disorganized attachment. This fourth style emerged in infants who lacked a clear strategy to cope with separation and reunion, often due to traumatic experiences or neglect. This discovery highlighted the intricate dance between early life events and attachment patterns, revealing the intricate emotional threads that weave the fabric of human development.

The collective contributions of Bowlby, Ainsworth, and their contemporaries have left an indelible mark on the field of psychology. Their work shattered existing boundaries and ignited a paradigm shift in understanding the profound significance of early caregiving in shaping emotional growth over a lifetime.

As we journey through the paths paved by these pioneering minds, we grasp the enduring impact of attachment theory. It's a narrative of audacious thinkers who challenged norms, embarked on groundbreaking research journeys, and unveiled the layers of human emotional development. The evolutionary perspective brought forth by Bowlby and the meticulous empirical approach of Ainsworth have provided us with a comprehensive lens to comprehend the intricate dance between infants and their caregivers. This narrative is one of transformation, an ongoing story that continues to reshape our understanding of love, care, and the emotional bonds that form in the earliest stages of life.

In these insights, we discover the seeds of understanding that bloom into the complex garden of relationships, offering us a deeper awareness of the roots that anchor our connections and the potential for nurturing profound emotional growth throughout our lives.

NOTES

NOTES

NOTES

NOTES

2

Deciphering Adult Attachment

In the journey of understanding attachment, we cast a spotlight on the fascinating world of adult attachment patterns. While the origins of attachment theory lie in infant and child relationships, researchers soon discovered that these patterns weave themselves into our grown-up lives. This revelation sparked a wave of exploration, diving into the dynamics of attachment in adolescents and adults, even stretching to the intergenerational threads that connect generations.

A tapestry woven through time, connecting the dots between our earliest years and the relationships we build as adults. Here we unravels the complexities of adult attachment patterns, inviting us to explore the intricate web that binds our emotional connections.

Attachment Stability and Change:

Picture a long corridor stretching from infancy to adulthood, lined with studies that meticulously track participants through the years. These studies unveil a captivating truth: attachment styles show a certain stability over time, but they're far from being set in stone. Waters et al. (2000) discovered that a substantial 72% of infants maintained their attachment style into adulthood. However, the journey isn't fixed. Life's twists and turns, the major events that shape us, can sway our attachment security. Trauma might deepen insecurities while nurturing relationships can pave the way for a more secure bond. For instance, a child who experienced neglect or inconsistent caregiving early in life might develop an anxious attachment style, always seeking validation and reassurance due to the fear of abandonment. On the other hand, a child who witnessed conflict or emotional turmoil between caregivers might develop an avoidant attachment style, learning to suppress emotions and maintain distance as a way to protect themselves from getting hurt.

This dynamic dance between continuity and fluidity paints a vivid portrait of how we evolve through our lifespan. Just as the roots of our attachment patterns are often traced back to early experiences, our ongoing interactions and relationships can shape and reshape these patterns over time. For instance, a person who had a secure attachment with their parents but experiences a traumatic event later in life might find their secure foundation shaken, leading to heightened anxiety and hypervigilance in relationships.

Conversely, a person who grew up with an insecure attachment style might embark on a journey of healing through therapy or supportive relationships. As they develop a deeper understanding of their attachment patterns, they begin to challenge their automatic responses and explore new ways of relating. Through consistent and positive experiences in relationships, they can gradually shift towards a more secure bond.

This dynamic interplay between early experiences and ongoing interactions underscores the malleability of attachment patterns. While our early attachments provide a foundation, they are not fixed in stone. The fluidity of attachment styles offers hope and potential for growth, transformation, and healing. As we navigate life's challenges and joys, we continue to shape our attachment narrative, rewriting its script as we learn, heal, and connect with ourselves and others.

Understanding Adult Attachment

Now, let's zoom in on how psychologists dissect adult attachment. Imagine two dimensions, like coordinates on a map, guiding us through the labyrinth of human connections. One axis measures attachment anxiety - the degree to which we worry about relationships. The other axis gauges attachment avoidance - our inclination to avoid emotional closeness. These dimensions give birth to four distinct adult attachment styles, much like those seen in childhood:

Secure: Low on anxiety and avoidance, these individuals find a balance between intimacy and independence. They're like the steady anchors in relationships, fostering healthy connections.

Anxious: High on anxiety, these individuals might grapple with worries of rejection or abandonment. Their emotions can sway like a pendulum, leading to intense highs and lows.

Avoidant: High on avoidance, these individuals are cautious about emotional closeness. They might lean toward self-sufficiency and find it challenging to fully open up.

Disorganized: This fourth category, akin to a rare gem, emerges from a mix of anxiety and avoidance. It's like having conflicting emotional scripts, resulting in unpredictable patterns.

Bartholomew's Insightful Model

Now, let's journey deeper into the realm of relationships. Picture a sculptor shaping a statue, chiselling away at the marble to reveal intricate details. Bartholomew did just that with attachment styles, adding a layer of depth. He envisioned four statues representing attachment styles:

Secure: These individuals have a positive outlook on themselves and others, creating a sturdy foundation for healthy relationships. For example, imagine a person who grew up in a household where caregivers were consistently responsive to their needs. This person internalized a sense of worthiness and trust in their relationships. As an adult, they approach connections with a sense of security, feeling comfortable both giving and receiving affection. They are able to express their needs openly while respecting the autonomy of their partners. This secure base allows them to navigate conflicts with empathy and effectively communicate, fostering a harmonious and fulfilling bond.

Preoccupied: These individuals have a negative self-image, seeking affirmation from others. They're like a puzzle piece that fits only when surrounded by someone else's validation. For instance, a person who experienced inconsistent caregiving during childhood. They might have learned to doubt their own worthiness and constantly seek external reassurance to fill the void left by their early experiences. In relationships, they may exhibit clinginess and fears of abandonment, often becoming preoccupied with their partner's actions and seeking constant affirmation. Their quest for validation can sometimes lead to overdependence and anxieties, as they struggle to find a stable sense of self without external approval. This attachment style may prompt them to interpret even minor disagreements as signs of rejection, further reinforcing their insecurities.

Dismissive: Here, a positive self-image coexists with skepticism about others. It's like holding the keys to the castle while raising the drawbridge to keep others out. Consider an individual who grew up in an environment where emotional expression was discouraged or dismissed. They learned to rely on themselves for emotional support and developed a self-sufficient attitude. As an adult, they may value their independence and have a strong sense of self-worth. However, they might struggle with opening up to others and allowing themselves to be vulnerable. In relationships, they may keep their partners at arm's length, avoiding deep emotional connections. Their skepticism about others' intentions can lead to a reluctance to rely on or trust others, creating a dynamic where they maintain control over their emotional world while avoiding the risk of being hurt.

Fearful: These individuals are wrestling with negative self-perception and distrust for others. It's like a dance between longing for connection and fearing it at the same time. Imagine a person who experienced inconsistent and even abusive caregiving during childhood. They might have internalized conflicting messages about their worthiness and the reliability of others. As adults, they find themselves torn between a deep desire for emotional closeness and an intense fear of being hurt again. In relationships, they may exhibit unpredictable behavior, alternating between seeking intimacy and pushing others away out of fear of being rejected or harmed. Their attachment style might manifest as a push-pull dynamic, where they simultaneously crave connection while fearing the potential pain it might bring. This complex dance of emotions can lead to intense relationship struggles as they navigate their inner turmoil and external relationships simultaneously.

Assessment and Impact

Let's switch gears to the tools researchers use to uncover these attachment patterns. Think of interviews, self-reports, and observation as our trusty navigational tools. By understanding our attachment style through these methods, we gain insights into the inner workings of our relationships. These assessment tools provide us with a map to navigate the intricate terrain of human connections.

When it comes to interviews, the Adult Attachment Interview (AAI) stands as a cornerstone. Self-report questionnaires, such as the Experiences in Close Relationships (ECR) and Attachment Style Questionnaire (ASQ), invite us to reflect on our emotions and behavior in relationships, helping us piece together the puzzle of our attachment tendencies.

Observational methods, on the other hand, offer a front-row seat to the dynamics of our attachments. Just like watching the tides of the ocean, observing infants in the Strange Situation or analyzing adults' interactions with their partners provides glimpses into the ebb and flow of our emotional connections.
We will delve deeper into these assessment tools in chapter 4

But why do we bother with this navigation? Because attachment doesn't just stop at influencing who we're close to; it shapes how we function in these connections. Research reveals that attachment styles leave their mark on the quality of our relationships and even our mental health.

The knowledge of our attachment tendencies serves as a compass, guiding us toward personal growth and thriving connections. By understanding how our past experiences influence our present behavior, we gain the power to rewrite our relational narratives.

We've embarked on a journey into the heart of adult attachment, a landscape shaped by the roots of our earliest bonds. The discoveries unearthed here remind us that we're not simply isolated individuals; we're interconnected beings, with the threads of attachment weaving a tapestry of emotions, behaviours, and connections that stretch across the canvas of our lives. As we move forward, let's remember that our attachment styles are not just a blueprint of the past; they hold the key to crafting richer, more fulfilling relationships and nurturing our emotional well-being.

NOTES

NOTES

NOTES

3

How Our Attachment Styles Shape How We Connect and Thrive

Imagine a vast landscape of research, where countless studies have unveiled an astonishing truth: the attachment styles we develop in childhood don't simply fade away as we grow older. Instead, they weave themselves into the very fabric of our being, influencing how we see ourselves and our relationships as adults.

Let's explore the profound impacts of these attachment styles on various dimensions of our lives:

1. Shaping Our Self-Concept:

Ever wondered how you perceive yourself? Attachment style holds the key. Studies have shown that individuals with a secure attachment tend to view themselves more positively, boasting higher self-esteem and a healthy self-image. On the flip side, those with insecure attachment styles, such as anxious or avoidant, might grapple with feelings of unworthiness or struggle to find confidence. Imagine how this influence from our earliest years can echo throughout our lives, influencing how we perceive our own worth and capabilities.

2. Guiding Our Emotions and Worldviews:
Picture your emotions as a compass guiding you through life. Attachment style plays a role in shaping this compass. Securely attached individuals often see the world as a place of comfort and safety. They're more adept at handling their emotions and finding balance. Meanwhile, anxious attachment might lead to a more pessimistic view of relationships and heightened emotional swings, while avoidant attachment might make someone less trusting and more inclined to suppress emotions. These dynamics showcase how attachment styles can tint our worldview and colour our emotional experiences.

3. Influencing Our Relationship Dynamics:
Relationships are the tapestry of our lives, and attachment styles wield a significant brush in their creation. Securely attached individuals tend to excel at communication, offering support to partners, and striking a balance between intimacy and independence. On the other hand, anxiously attached individuals might grapple with insecurities, leading to possessiveness and constant reassurance-seeking. Avoidantly attached individuals might have a harder time with emotional intimacy, potentially isolating themselves. The impact of disorganized attachment might result in erratic relationship patterns, revealing how our early bonds continue to shape our connections.

4. Linking to Mental Health:
The influence of attachment doesn't stop at our relationships; it stretches into the realm of our mental well-being. Secure attachment acts like a shield, promoting resilience and emotional stability. In contrast, insecure attachment styles heighten the risk of mental health challenges like depression, anxiety, post-traumatic stress disorder

(PTSD), and personality disorders. This insight underscores the importance of understanding how attachment history can intersect with our emotional health.

We've delved into a profound realization: our attachment styles are like guiding scripts, influencing how we see ourselves, interact with others, and handle life's challenges. The attachment patterns we develop in our early years are not just stories of the past; they are the building blocks of our emotional landscape as adults.

The implications are clear: awareness matters. Recognizing the influence of our attachment styles empowers us to make conscious choices in how we perceive ourselves, approach relationships, and manage our emotions. The journey of self-discovery we embark upon when understanding our attachment styles can lead to transformative growth, enriching our connections with others and nurturing our emotional well-being.

As we move forward in our exploration, let's keep in mind that our attachment styles are a map we've carried with us since childhood. In the chapters ahead, we'll unveil strategies and insights to navigate this map, fostering healthier relationships, fostering personal growth, and harnessing the power of our emotional history to shape a brighter future.

NOTES

NOTES

NOTES

4

Decoding Attachment

Let us delve into the tools researchers have crafted to help us uncover our attachment styles, shedding light on our thoughts, emotions, and behaviours in relationships. These tools are like treasure maps guiding us through the labyrinth of our emotional landscape. However, it's important to note that while these tools provide valuable insights, they come with their own set of limitations that should be handled with care.

Imagine a toolkit brimming with methods designed to uncover the mysteries of our attachment styles. These methods provide a window into our relational world, helping us piece together the puzzle of how we bond with others.

1. Self-Report Measures:

Think of these as questionnaires that we fill out about ourselves. They ask us to reflect on our feelings, thoughts, and behaviors in relationships. For example, the "Experiences in Close Relationships" (ECR) questionnaire asks about how anxious or avoidant we feel in romantic connections. Imagine being presented with questions like,

"When my partner is away, I worry that they might not come back," or "I prefer not to rely on others for support." These questions give us a glimpse into our emotional responses and attachment tendencies in relationships.

Another tool in this category is the "Attachment Style Questionnaire" (ASQ). This questionnaire takes us on a journey through different attachment styles, asking us to assess statements like, "I find it easy to trust others," "I often feel uncomfortable when someone gets too close," and "I sometimes worry that people I care about might leave me." These questions invite us to explore the core of our attachment behaviors, revealing whether we lean towards being secure, anxious, avoidant, or even disorganized in our connections.

It's important to keep in mind that these questionnaires rely on our own perceptions and self-awareness. Just as a photograph captures a single moment, these self-report measures capture a snapshot of our emotional landscape. However, our self-perceptions can be influenced by our past experiences, beliefs, and even our mood on the day we fill out the questionnaire. That's why, while these tools provide valuable insights, they are just one piece of the larger puzzle of understanding our attachment style.

2. Interview Assessments:

Let's picture a scenario where you're sitting across from a skilled detective, not for solving crimes, but for unraveling the mysteries of your attachment experiences. Interview assessments are like having a deep and meaningful conversation with someone who genuinely wants to understand your emotional journey. One of these interviews is called the "Adult Attachment Interview" (AAI). It's like a marathon dialogue where you talk about your relationships in childhood, digging into memories and feelings. It's often considered the gold standard for understanding attachment, but here's the catch: it requires time and the expertise of professionals who can carefully analyze your responses.

Now, imagine another type of interview that focuses on your romantic relationships or your thoughts about being a parent. These interviews are like having a heart-to-heart conversation with someone who's interested in your experiences and emotions. They ask questions that prompt you to reflect on your attachment-related thoughts and behaviors.

These interview assessments provide a deeper layer of understanding compared to self-report measures. They help us explore the intricate details of our attachment history and how it has shaped our present relationships. However, just like a detective needs to interpret clues, these interviews require skilled interpreters who can decode the emotional nuances hidden within our stories. They help us connect the dots between our past and our current patterns of relating.

3. Observation Methods:

RPicture researchers peeking into our lives, watching us interact with others. They might observe infants and caregivers in the "Strange Situation" or analyze how adults behave with their romantic partners in a lab setting. They could even study the way we use language to uncover hidden attachment themes. These methods give us an external perspective on our relationships, showing how we connect when we might not even realize we're being watched.

However, as we use these tools to unearth the hidden treasures of our attachment styles, it's essential to be aware of their limitations and the ethical considerations that come with them.

Self-reports might not tell the whole story. They rely on how we perceive ourselves, which can sometimes be coloured by our own biases or the way we think we "should" feel. Interviews are rich sources of information, but they need skilled professionals to decode the complexities of our narratives.

Context matters. Our attachment behaviours can shift based on the situation we're in. We might behave differently with friends, family, and romantic partners.

Categories can be confining. Human emotions are complex and can't always be neatly fit into categories like secure, anxious, avoidant, or disorganized. The richness of our emotional landscape often transcends these labels.

Ethics are crucial. These tools should be used ethically and responsibly, guided by experts who understand their nuances. Uncovering attachment styles can bring up deep emotions, and it's important to ensure individuals are supported throughout the process.

We've peeled back the curtain on the methods that researchers use to reveal the inner workings of our attachment styles. These tools offer us a unique opportunity to glimpse into our emotional world, to understand our tendencies in relationships better, and to navigate the intricate pathways of our emotional history.

As we move forward in our exploration, let's remember that these tools are like compasses guiding us through the landscapes of our connections. With the right guidance and insight, we can harness the power of these tools to enrich our relationships, foster personal growth, and journey toward a more profound understanding of ourselves and our emotional bonds.

NOTES

NOTES

NOTES

5

Building Stronger Bonds

The pathways to achieving more stable and fulfilling relationships are illuminated, demonstrating that change is not only possible but attainable with dedication and effort.

A question often asked is whether our attachment styles are set in stone or if change is possible.Some researchers are suggesting that these patterns are etched in time, while others propose that change is a journey we can embark upon at any point in life. Studies have shown that life's events can indeed influence the way we perceive relationships. Notably significant connections can lead to what's called "earned security," a gradual evolution towards a more secure attachment style. Therapy, too, plays a role in facilitating change, although it's essential to note that progress is a steady and gradual process. Here, motivation becomes the guiding star, the driving force that fuels the journey towards transformation.

Techniques for Nurturing Security

Imagine stepping onto a path of self-discovery and growth, armed with techniques that can reshape the very fabric of your connections.

If you're eager to embark on this journey, there are strategies that can pave the way:

Psychotherapy Approaches: Imagine finding yourself in a warm and supportive environment, a space where your emotional wounds and needs are met with understanding and compassion. Psychotherapy approaches like Emotionally Focused Therapy, Circle of Security, and Dyadic Developmental Psychotherapy provide this kind of space for healing and growth. It's like embarking on a journey of self-discovery and transformation.

These psychotherapy approaches offer a safe space where you can explore your attachment history, understand the impact of your past on your present relationships, and develop new strategies for building secure bonds. It's like having a toolkit to mend old wounds and create healthier patterns of connection.

Mindfulness Practices: a practice that acts as a gentle lantern, illuminating the intricate pathways of your emotions. Mindfulness is like a guide that helps you navigate through the labyrinth of your feelings with grace and presence.

Mindfulness practices encourage you to be fully present in the moment, to experience each sensation, thought, and emotion as it arises. It's like giving yourself permission to pause and listen to the whispers of your own heart. Through this practice, you become more attuned to your inner landscape, gaining insight into your attachment patterns and how they influence your interactions with others.

Just as a lantern guides you through a dark forest, mindfulness guides you through the complexities of your emotions. It's a tool that empowers you to respond to challenging situations with greater clarity and compassion. Like a gentle companion, mindfulness supports you in developing a deeper understanding of yourself and your attachment journey.

Communication and Interpersonal Skills: Envision embarking on a journey of learning a new dance, one that transforms the way you connect with others. It's like rewiring the familiar steps you've taken in your relationships, replacing them with healthier and more harmonious movements that foster understanding and deep connection.

Communication and interpersonal skills are like mastering the steps of an intricate dance. You practice empathy, putting yourself in another's shoes, and responding with kindness. It's like offering a hand to lead your partner through a complicated sequence. Through these skills, you create a space for mutual understanding and shared vulnerability.

Just as a dance requires coordination and practice, improving your communication and interpersonal skills involves effort and intention. It's about nurturing a dialogue that encourages authentic expression and active listening. With each step you take in this new dance, you nurture connections that are rooted in empathy, respect, and genuine engagement.

Cultivating Self-Compassion: Picture a transformation within your inner world, as if you're replacing a relentless critic with a gentle and understanding friend. This shift in how you perceive yourself becomes a powerful tool, like a guiding light that helps you navigate the labyrinth of attachment patterns.

Cultivating self-compassion is like a practice where you consciously choose to treat yourself with kindness and understanding. It's recognizing that just like everyone else, you have your own vulnerabilities and imperfections. Instead of berating yourself for them, you offer yourself the same care you would offer a dear friend.

Imagine a day when you stumble and make a mistake. Instead of the usual self-criticism, you hear a gentle voice within, acknowledging that everyone stumbles at times. It's like a friend extending a hand to help you up, reminding you that setbacks are part of the human experience.

Cultivating self-compassion rewires the way you relate to yourself, influencing the way you connect with others. As you replace self-criticism with self-kindness, you also extend that kindness to those around you. It's like a ripple effect that spreads empathy and understanding, creating an environment of acceptance and healing.

Through this practice, you transform your inner landscape and, in turn, reshape the dynamics of your relationships.

Taking Calculated Risks: Imagine standing at the edge of your comfort zone, where the familiar gives way to the unknown. It's like a threshold of growth, and with each step beyond, you venture into uncharted territory. This is where the magic of change unfolds, and acting in ways that challenge your avoidant or anxious tendencies becomes a powerful catalyst.

Consider an individual accustomed to avoiding emotional vulnerability, a protective strategy built over time. Now, imagine them taking a deep breath and sharing their feelings openly with a loved one. The act is akin to planting a seed of change in the soil of connection. It might feel uneasy at first, like treading on unfamiliar ground, but with each honest conversation, the soil becomes more fertile, nurturing the growth of healthier bonds.

Taking calculated risks is not about recklessness but a mindful and intentional choice. It's about recognizing that growth often requires stepping into the discomfort zone. Imagine a person grappling with social anxiety who decides to attend a social gathering. The anticipation might stir unease, but by facing the discomfort head-on, they gradually build confidence and reshape their relationship with social interactions.

Just as an athlete pushes their limits to become stronger, taking calculated risks in the realm of attachment fosters emotional resilience. It's like forging a new pathway through the wilderness of fear and avoidance, one step at a time. Each risk you take, each moment of vulnerability you embrace, becomes a milestone of growth.

As you venture beyond the confines of what's familiar, you create room for change and transformation. The discomfort you feel is a sign that you're challenging the boundaries that have held you back. It's a testament to your courage and your commitment to evolving into a more secure and empowered version of yourself.

Expressing Attachment Needs: Envision a scenario where your unspoken needs are like locked treasures hidden within you. Now, picture yourself holding the key to unlock those treasures and share them with someone you care about. This act of vulnerability becomes a bridge that connects you on a deeper level, paving the way for greater understanding and intimacy.

Consider a person who has always been self-reliant, hesitant to ask for support or space when needed. Now, imagine them speaking up and sharing their need for alone time to recharge. It's like a beacon illuminating their emotional landscape, allowing those around them to navigate their inner terrain with greater sensitivity.

Expressing attachment needs is not a sign of weakness, but a display of emotional courage. It's like extending a hand and saying, "This is who I am, and this is what I long for in our relationship." When you share your needs, you offer a glimpse into your heart, fostering a space where understanding and empathy can thrive.

Voicing attachment needs requires vulnerability, as you open yourself to the possibility of rejection or misunderstanding. But within that vulnerability lies the potential for deeper connection. It's like crossing a bridge that connects two worlds – your world and the world of your loved one. As you cross that bridge, you invite them to meet you halfway, creating a space where your emotional needs can be acknowledged and met.

Setting New Goals: Envision standing at the crossroads of transformation, armed with a personalized roadmap to guide your journey. Just as a traveler plans their route, you too can chart a course towards personal growth using S.M.A.R.T goals. These goals are like signposts that lead you away from old patterns and towards the horizon of change.

S.M.A.R.T stands for Specific, Measurable, Achievable, Relevant, and Time-bound. Imagine each of these qualities as a cornerstone of your journey, providing structure and direction.

Consider a person who wishes to enhance their communication skills within their relationships. They decide to set a S.M.A.R.T goal: "I will actively practice listening to my partner's thoughts and feelings for at least 10 minutes every day for the next month."

Specific: The goal is clearly defined – the individual aims to improve their listening skills.

Measurable: The progress is quantifiable – they will spend a dedicated 10 minutes daily engaging in active listening.

Achievable: The goal is realistic – devoting 10 minutes a day is feasible within their schedule.

Relevant: The goal is aligned with their aspirations – enhancing communication directly contributes to building healthier relationships.

Time-bound: The goal has a set timeframe – they commit to practicing for a month.

Setting S.M.A.R.T goals is a commitment to your own growth. It's like crafting a compass that directs you towards the change you seek. With each goal achieved, you move closer to transforming your attachment patterns and fostering deeper, more meaningful connections. Just as a traveler takes one step at a time, you too can embrace the journey of change, knowing that every step counts.

Steps Towards Secure Bonds

The path towards security involves joint efforts. For couples, joint counselling becomes a space to foster vulnerability, responsiveness to needs, empathy, and emotional availability. It's like tending to a garden of emotions, nurturing growth through shared understanding.

In parenting, caregivers responding sensitively and consistently to a child's needs, modelling healthy connections, and offering a blend of support and autonomy become the architects of secure bonds.

Though the journey towards secure attachments might seem challenging, envision the rewards that await. With motivation and a support system, we have the power to rewrite old scripts, transform dynamics, and cultivate more secure connections at any stage of life. It's a journey that holds the promise of stronger relationships, deeper self-understanding, and a richer emotional tapestry that unfolds with every step.

Let's remember that change is a journey of intention and courage. The keys to a more secure attachment style are within our grasp, and with each step we take, we inch closer to the rewards that lie ahead.

NOTES

NOTES

NOTES

NOTES

6

Unlocking the Brain's Role in Attachment

Imagine the human brain as a grand symphony hall, where intricate melodies of emotions and relationships reverberate through the corridors of our consciousness. This captivating symphony is conducted by a profound biological blueprint, a symphony conductor directing the complex interplay of our biology and our bonds. This mesmerizing composition is a result of years of meticulous research into brain development and physiology, gradually revealing the profound connections that exist between our neural intricacies and the depth of our human connections.

In this metaphorical symphony, each neuron represents a musician, each firing synapse a note, and each neural pathway a harmonious arrangement. As researchers delve into the intricate score of our brain's blueprint, they illuminate the symphony's most delicate nuances, showing how our brain processes and responds to the bonds we form with others.

The release of oxytocin and dopamine, for example, can be likened to crescendos of emotional resonance and bonding. These biological players are the secret instruments behind the scenes, creating the harmonious chords of attachment that resonate deep within us.

As studies unfold, it becomes evident that certain brain regions orchestrate the symphony's most pivotal moments. Components of the limbic system and the brain's reward pathways light up like spotlight beams as they come to life during moments of connection. Imagine a mother gazing into her infant's eyes – in that exchange, the brain's intricate ensemble is in full harmony, the symphony of attachment resounding.

Securely attached individuals might have a well-practiced melody of trust and emotional regulation, while those with insecure attachment patterns may experience a discordant tune of anxiety or avoidance.

With every discovery, researchers gain a deeper understanding of the brain's role in shaping our relationships. This evolving symphony of knowledge not only enhances our comprehension of attachment but also illuminates the interconnectedness of our human experience.

This symphony of science and sentiment offers a new lens through which to marvel at the intricate choreography that unites us in the dance of attachment.

The Hormonal Harmony of Attachment

Imagine the rush of emotions when you're close to someone you care about. That rush is fueled by a hormonal symphony within us. Research has revealed that forming attachments triggers the release of key hormones, acting as messengers that shape our connections.

- Oxytocin:this hormone is the "bonding molecule." When released, it fosters feelings of trust and connection. It's like the glue that holds us close to those we love, nurturing our emotional ties.
Oxytocin is a remarkable hormone that plays a significant role in the bonds we form with others, as well as in some of life's most intimate and profound experiences.

When a mother gives birth brain experiences a surge of oxytocin, akin to a crescendo of emotion and connection. This hormonal release serves to strengthen the bond between the mother and her newborn, promoting feelings of attachment and caregiving.

But the symphony of oxytocin doesn't end there. It also takes center stage during another deeply personal experience: orgasm. Oxytocin is released during orgasm, creating a euphoric and intimate connection between individuals. This release is weaving together pleasure, connection, and emotional depth in a harmonious blend.

Whether it's the gentle embrace of a new mother and her baby or the passionate connection between lovers, oxytocin adds its unique notes to the symphony of attachment, reminding us of the intricate ways our biology shapes our most cherished bonds.

Dopamine : often referred to as the "reward molecule," is like a cheerful performer in the grand theater of our brain. It takes the spotlight when moments of pleasure, satisfaction, and reward unfold in our lives. Dopamine lights up our brain's stage when we experience something pleasurable or fulfilling.

When you achieve a goal, savor a delicious meal, or engage in an enjoyable activity, dopamine takes center stage, creating a sensation of delight. It's as if the brain is sending a resounding round of applause, signaling that something wonderful has happened. This surge of dopamine serves as a biological high-five, reinforcing the behavior that led to the positive experience.

When we form deep connections with others, whether through close friendships, romantic relationships, or nurturing family bonds, dopamine becomes an essential partner in an emotional waltz. Every shared laugh, heartfelt conversation, or tender moment triggers a release of dopamine, infusing the experience with a sense of reward and pleasure.

As we cultivate bonds with loved ones, the brain remembers these moments of connection and the accompanying dopamine releases. This creates a loop of positive reinforcement: the brain associates being around certain individuals with feelings of happiness and reward. It's like the brain's way of saying, "This person makes you feel good, so keep them close."

Whether it's the laughter shared with a friend, the warmth of a loved one's embrace, or the bliss of an intimate moment, dopamine adds its euphoric notes to the soundtrack of our emotional connections, reminding us that the bonds we build are intrinsically linked to the sensations of reward and happiness.

The Brain's Choreography of Attachment

Studies using FMRI (functional magnetic resonance imaging) have revealed that specific brain regions and pathways spring to life when, for instance, a mother gazes at her infant. This dance takes place in the limbic system and reward pathways, regions responsible for processing emotions and pleasure.

Secure Attachment and Brain Growth

Studies have shown that children with secure attachments tend to experience greater development in vital brain regions. Think of the hippocampus, a region linked to stress modulation, as the compass guiding us through life's challenges. Insecure attachments, on the other hand, have been linked to impacts on the frontal lobe's executive functions, which play a role in decision-making, problem-solving, and emotional regulation.

A Symphony of Care and Development

Now, let's imagine the heartwarming scenes of attentive parents caring for their infants. This care, it turns out, isn't just an emotional act; it's a symphony that shapes a child's social development and stress-handling abilities. Picture parents as conductors of this symphony, nurturing the intricate melodies of their child's growth.

Remember that the brain isn't just a complex organ; it's a canvas on which our relationships are painted. The pathways of biology and emotion intertwine, crafting the symphony of attachment that we experience. This chapter has illuminated how our bonds are more than just feelings; they're a dance orchestrated by our brains, a dance that shapes our connections, moulds our growth, and paves the way for a lifetime of emotional resonance.

NOTES

NOTES

NOTES

7

Threads of Attachment Across Cultures

Consider attachment theory as a foundational concept that was initially rooted in the Western world. Over time, this concept has grown and branched out, much like a tree extending its limbs in various directions. As these branches stretch towards different cultures, they encounter the unique influences of cultural values, beliefs, and norms. This interplay between attachment theory and cultural contexts creates a diverse and intricate landscape of emotional bonds and relational dynamics.

Just as diverse climates give rise to a variety of ecosystems, different cultures cultivate distinct ways of forming and maintaining emotional connections.

Imagine a tapestry woven from threads of attachment theory and cultural intricacies. Each thread contributes to the intricate patterns that emerge, reflecting the specific values and norms of a given culture. These cultural weaves influence how individuals perceive closeness, express affection, and navigate dependency within relationships.

In one culture, attachment may be emphasized through strong family ties and collective responsibility for caregiving. In another, individual autonomy might take precedence, influencing how emotional needs are communicated and met. These cultural nuances shape the very fabric of attachment bonds, giving rise to diverse attachment styles and patterns.

Rather than a one-size-fits-all approach, attachment theory recognizes the importance of considering these cultural weaves. It acknowledges that attachment is not solely a universal concept, but one that takes on rich and varied forms across different cultural contexts. Exploring attachment through a cultural lens is like delving into a mosaic of human experiences, where each piece contributes to a broader understanding of how attachment thrives and evolves within diverse societies.

Cultural Influences on Caregiving

Consider the cultural influences on caregiving as a spectrum that spans across diverse landscapes. In one scene, you witness the intricate dance of an extended family coming together to nurture a child, each member contributing their unique role. In another scene, the focus shifts to parents as the primary caregivers, their responsibilities concentrated within the nucleus of the family unit. These scenes paint a vivid picture of how culture shapes the very foundations of caregiving norms.

In collectivist cultures: extended family members intertwine to create a safety net of support for the child. The strength of these interwoven threads becomes a symbol of communal responsibility, where caregiving is a shared effort.

The child is embraced by the warmth of a larger network, and the process of growing up is a collective endeavor.

In individualistic societies: Here, the focus is on the nuclear family unit as the primary source of care, and the threads that compose this tapestry are meticulously intertwined between parents. The child's upbringing is a reflection of close-knit familial bonds that prioritize autonomy and independence.

Both scenes demonstrate the intricate ways in which cultural values shape the role and scope of caregiving. Collectivist cultures celebrate the strength of unity, where caregiving is a shared responsibility carried by multiple generations. In contrast, individualistic societies emphasize the autonomy of the immediate family, where parents play a central role in nurturing their children.

These cultural influences become the soil in which caregiving norms take root, nurturing the growth of attachment bonds in distinct and meaningful ways. Through this lens, we glimpse the rich diversity of caregiving practices that enrich the tapestry of human experiences across cultures.

Separation

Different societies handle separation from caregivers based on values about dependence and independence. In some cultures, fostering early independence is celebrated, while in others, attachment is nurtured by close physical proximity.

Attachments Across Borders

Sensitive caregiving, characterized by responsiveness and warmth, is the common thread that nurtures secure bonds. However, the meaning of behaviours that constitute sensitive caregiving can vary from culture to culture. A soothing touch might be universally nurturing, but its meaning within a cultural context can differ.

Cultural Biases and Assessment Tools

Assessment tools are cultural lenses through which we view attachment. These lenses can sometimes blur our vision, emphasizing constructs that may not align with every cultural context. For instance, the concept of separation anxiety might not resonate the same way across cultures. It's like a language that speaks louder in some cultures than in others.

Unraveling Cultural Complexities

Cross-cultural research is an explorer's map, guiding us through uncharted territories. It's a journey that's vital for understanding the intricate interplay between cultural contexts and universal developmental needs. As we learn from diverse cultures, we uncover the threads that weave us together and the nuances that set us apart.

The tapestry of attachment isn't confined by borders; it's a mosaic of cultural influences. Our emotional connections are influenced by the cultures we're woven into, and understanding these threads enriches our comprehension of the human experience. With each step we take on this cross-cultural journey, we honor the diversity of caregiving practices, celebrate the common human need for attachment, and continue weaving a global narrative of connection and care.

NOTES

NOTES

NOTES

NOTES

8

Weaving Attachment into Real Life

We now find ourselves at the intersection of theory and practice, where the insights of attachment theory are woven into the fabric of everyday life. Imagine these insights as guiding stars that illuminate the path for parenting, education, mental health, and caregiving. We now embark on a journey where the wisdom of attachment theory is translated into tangible actions that shape the lives of individuals, families, and communities.

Fostering Emotional Security

At its core, attachment theory shines as a guiding light, illuminating the intricate pathways that weave through our relationships. Its essence revolves around a fundamental yet deeply impactful insight: that consistent and sensitive caregiving serves as the fertile soil for cultivating emotional security. This theory is like a beacon that directs us through the labyrinth of human connections, offering a clear perspective on how our interactions shape our sense of safety and trust.

Caregivers who grasp the principles of attachment theory provide an emotional radiance that bathes their loved ones in a sense of well-being.

Attachment theory underscores the importance of caregivers tuning into the cues of those they care for.

Attachment theory reminds us that the quality of our connections directly influences our emotional landscapes. This theory invites us to cultivate an awareness of our interactions, to understand that the way we respond to attachment cues shapes the emotional terrain of those around us.

In essence, attachment theory is an invitation to embrace the role of emotional gardeners in the lives of our loved ones. By tending to their attachment needs, we create an environment where trust, safety, and understanding can flourish. This theory reminds us that our actions as caregivers have the power to sow the seeds of emotional security, ultimately leading to a harvest of thriving relationships and resilient hearts.

Empowering Parents with Knowledge

Attachment theory serves as a guidebook for parents, enabling them to decipher the intricate language of their children's emotions. Through parent education programs rooted in attachment research, caregivers are empowered to understand and respond to the subtle cues that children employ to express their attachment needs. It's akin to acquiring a universal language that deepens the connection between parent and child.

For instance, imagine a young child who clings to their parent when faced with a new environment. This behavior becomes an emotional cue, a gentle whisper of their need for reassurance and comfort. Through the lens of attachment theory, parents become adept at recognizing such cues. They understand that this clinging is more than just a reaction to the unfamiliar; it's a reflection of the child's desire for the secure presence of their caregiver.

Similarly, consider a teenager who withdraws and becomes quiet after a challenging day. This emotional cue, though subtle, signals a need for understanding and support. Armed with the insights of attachment theory, parents can approach the situation with empathy, acknowledging the underlying emotions that the teenager may not be overtly expressing.

Attachment theory provides parents with a toolkit to navigate these emotional cues effectively. It's like deciphering a code that unlocks the door to their children's hearts. By responding to these cues, parents provide the emotional safety net that bolsters their children's confidence, resilience, and sense of security.

In essence, attachment theory acts as a bridge between parents and children, allowing them to communicate beyond words. It's a shared language that enhances the parent-child bond, fostering a relationship of trust, understanding, and mutual support. Just as travelers in a foreign land benefit from learning the local language, caregivers who embrace the insights of attachment theory become fluent in the emotional language of their children, enriching their journey of parenthood.

Nurturing Bonds in Challenging Times

In the realm of caregiving, particularly during challenging times, the principles of attachment serve as a steadfast anchor guiding professionals and caregivers alike. These principles not only encompass the prevention of harm but also encompass the delicate art of nurturing healthy bonds that withstand the trials of life. It's like constructing a safety net that not only safeguards individuals but also fosters the growth of emotional connections, even in the face of adversity.

Consider the way standard practices in abuse prevention are intricately woven with the threads of attachment theory. Beyond the immediate goal of ensuring safety, these practices are rooted in the broader mission of cultivating secure emotional bonds. It's akin to building a foundation that not only shields individuals from harm but also fosters a nurturing environment where relationships can thrive. Attachment theory becomes the blueprint that architects use to design resilient structures capable of weathering life's storms.

This safety net of attachment principles extends its protective embrace to children who find themselves in need of foster care or adoption. These children often carry with them a history of disrupted attachments, leaving them vulnerable to emotional wounds. In these circumstances, attachment measures emerge as invaluable tools, akin to compasses guiding professionals and caregivers through uncharted territories.

These attachment measures serve a dual purpose: they guide the selection of appropriate placements and also inform the design of personalized treatment plans. Each child's unique attachment needs are taken into account, just as an architect customizes a blueprint to fit the contours of the land. This tailored approach recognizes that the journey toward healing and security is a nuanced one, and that a one-size-fits-all approach would be inadequate.

Caregivers and professionals carefully select interventions and strategies to foster attachment security. It's a delicate dance that requires an understanding of each child's attachment history and needs. The goal is to create an environment that not only addresses past wounds but also nurtures the growth of healthy emotional bonds.

In essence, the principles of attachment provide a guiding light, a compass that helps caregivers and professionals navigate the intricate terrain of caregiving, even in the midst of challenging circumstances. These principles remind us that safety goes hand in hand with connection, that nurturing bonds is a crucial component of ensuring the well-being of those in our care.

Attachment in the Therapeutic Realm

In the realm of therapy, practitioners take on the role of skilled artisans, weaving intricate patterns using the threads of attachment theory to create a tapestry of healing. Like a weaver who selects each thread with care, therapists delve into the depths of attachment frameworks to unravel their clients' core relational patterns and uncover the unmet needs that lie beneath the surface. This process is akin to deciphering an emotional map that holds the key to understanding behavior and responses, revealing the intricate pathways that guide individuals through the landscape of their lives.

Therapist decipher the emotional clues that offer a glimpse into the hidden chambers of their clients' experiences, piecing together the puzzle of attachment dynamics that have shaped their journey thus far.

This insight isn't just a theoretical exercise; it's a compass that guides the therapeutic journey. Armed with a deep understanding of attachment patterns and their impact, therapists are better equipped to navigate the complex landscape of their clients' emotions, thoughts, and behaviors.

As therapists and clients embark on this journey together, the therapeutic space becomes a sanctuary where growth and change can unfold.

In this therapeutic tapestry, attachment theory threads its way through each session, weaving a narrative that helps clients make sense of their experiences. The framework of attachment provides a language for discussing emotions, a framework for exploring relationships, and a map for navigating the twists and turns of personal growth. It's like having a compass that points towards the true north of healing and flourishing.

Ultimately, the therapeutic journey is about more than just addressing symptoms; it's about uncovering the roots of those symptoms and fostering deep and lasting change. Therapists, armed with the insights of attachment theory, become guides who walk alongside their clients as they navigate the terrain of their emotions and relationships. With each step, therapists help clients rewrite their emotional narratives, cultivate healthier attachments, and embrace the possibility of a more fulfilling and authentic life.

Attachment-Aware Professionals

Social workers are like vigilant guardians armed with the knowledge of attachment theory. Equipped with specialized training, these professionals possess a unique lens through which they can perceive the intricacies of human relationships. It's as if they have been given a pair of glasses that allow them to see beyond the surface, enabling them to discern hidden patterns that hold the potential to significantly impact emotional development.

Imagine a social worker as a perceptive observer who can decipher the unspoken language of attachment dynamics. Just as a skilled detective spots clues that lead to hidden truths, social workers can identify subtle cues and behaviors that signal underlying attachment patterns. This keen awareness allows them to uncover the complex tapestry of emotions and experiences that shape an individual's relationship landscape.

Consider attachment theory as a guidebook that social workers carry in their toolkit. This guidebook doesn't just provide theoretical knowledge; it offers practical insights that can be applied to real-life situations. Social workers can identify when attachment dynamics are contributing to challenges or difficulties, allowing them to tailor their interventions to address these underlying patterns.

In essence, attachment theory empowers social workers to become architects of change within the lives of those they serve. Social workers design interventions and strategies that create supportive environments for individuals and families. They use the principles of attachment to construct frameworks that foster emotional security, resilience, and growth.

A Tapestry Across Contexts

Attachment theory is a versatile thread that weaves through various contexts. From parenting programs that lay the foundation for secure relationships, to schools that provide environments of emotional safety, attachment insights guide practices that nurture healthy bonds. In child services, the wisdom of attachment helps create brighter futures for those in challenging situations. And in mental health treatment, attachment theory offers a compass, directing therapists and clients towards a path of healing.

Remember that attachment theory isn't confined to textbooks; it's a living, breathing force that transforms lives. The insights we've explored are not just theoretical constructs; they're blueprints for action, tools for change, and beacons of hope. By bringing attachment theory into practice, we participate in a journey of connection, understanding, and growth that ripples through generations, shaping a world where relationships flourish and emotional security blossoms.

NOTES

NOTES

NOTES

NOTES

9

Healing Through Attachment-Informed Therapy

Therapy is a journey through the landscape of emotions and relationships. Now, overlay that with the wisdom of attachment theory, and you have the foundation for therapeutic interventions that spark change. These interventions are like keys that unlock doors long closed, paving the way for growth and healing.

Emotionally Focused Therapy: Rebuilding Trust

Emotionally Focused Therapy (EFT) is like having a skilled guide who helps you navigate the landscape of your emotions. It focuses on reshaping negative interaction patterns and fostering trust and responsiveness within relationships. It's about uncovering the root causes of your attachment-related struggles and learning new ways to build connection and intimacy.

Dyadic Developmental Psychotherapy: Nurturing Attachment and Healing Trauma

Dyadic Developmental Psychotherapy (DDP) is designed for individuals who have experienced high-risk backgrounds or trauma. It's like having a guide who walks alongside you as you navigate the path to healing. DDP focuses on creating a therapeutic relationship that mirrors healthy attachment dynamics. Through this relationship, individuals can experience corrective emotional experiences and find ways to heal their attachment wounds.

Circle of Security: Strengthening Bonds

Circle of Security is like having a mentor who supports you in nurturing healthy bonds, especially in relationships between parents and children. It's an early intervention program that empowers caregivers to understand and respond to their child's needs effectively. This approach helps create a secure foundation for children to grow emotionally and develop healthy attachment patterns.

Attachment Threads in Various Modalities

Picture a tapestry of therapeutic modalities woven with attachment principles. These threads are like golden lines connecting various approaches.

Eye Movement Desensitization and Reprocessing (EMDR) serves as a transformative tool for navigating the complex landscape of traumatic memories, all while integrating the principles of attachment theory.

This approach understands that these memories are not isolated fragments but are often intricately intertwined with attachment experiences. By addressing trauma through an attachment-focused lens, EMDR offers a comprehensive approach that acknowledges the profound impact of attachment dynamics on the healing process.

In this therapeutic journey, EMDR doesn't just focus on the traumatic memory itself; it also shines a light on the attachment-related emotions and patterns that might be interwoven with it. It's like untangling a knot, one strand at a time, until the threads of trauma and attachment are laid bare. By addressing both aspects, individuals are provided with a holistic healing experience that acknowledges the multifaceted nature of their emotional landscape.

For example, if a traumatic event involved a rupture in a significant relationship, EMDR helps you delve into the attachment-related emotions that emerged from that experience. Perhaps it triggered feelings of abandonment, fear, or mistrust. EMDR provides a safe space to process these emotions within the context of attachment, allowing you to address both the trauma itself and its implications for your relationships.

As you navigate this journey, EMDR acts as a bridge between past wounds and present healing. It recognizes that attachment dynamics can influence how traumatic memories are encoded and stored in the mind. By acknowledging the interplay between trauma and attachment, EMDR offers a unique opportunity to rewrite the emotional narrative associated with both

Dialectical Behavior Therapy (DBT) emerges as a beacon of guidance, providing individuals with a comprehensive toolkit to navigate the intricate landscape of emotions and interpersonal interactions. Like a skilled craftsman, DBT weaves together strategies for emotional regulation and interpersonal effectiveness, creating a tapestry of resilience and secure connections that stretches across the fabric of one's life.

This therapeutic approach recognizes that emotions can sometimes be tumultuous storms, threatening to erode the foundations of our well-being and relationships.

At the heart of DBT lies emotional regulation—a skill that empowers individuals to harness the power of their emotions rather than being swept away by them. Through mindfulness practices, distress tolerance techniques, and emotion modulation strategies, DBT provides the resources to navigate these emotional currents with intention and balance.

DBT imparts interpersonal effectiveness skills that empower individuals to traverse the delicate dynamics of relationships. These skills offer insights into effective communication, boundary setting, and conflict resolution, fostering an environment where connections can thrive and grow.

Someone who has undergone DBT, now equipped with emotional regulation techniques and interpersonal skills. They encounter moments of emotional turmoil, and instead of being overwhelmed, they draw upon their newfound knowledge to anchor themselves amidst the storm. This emotional mastery becomes the foundation upon which they build secure connections, as they communicate their needs, navigate conflicts, and foster empathy in their interactions.

Sensorimotor is a therapeutic approach that recognizes the profound connection between our bodies and our emotional well-being. This method taps into the body's innate wisdom, using the language of movement and awareness to mend the intricate fabric of attachment wounds.

Instead of solely relying on verbal communication, the individual engage in a dialogue with their body—a conversation that transcends words and delves into the realm of somatic sensations. This approach acknowledges that our bodies carry the imprints of our past experiences, like chapters etched into the fibers of our being.

Sensorimotor Psychotherapy understands that emotions often find their expression through our bodies.This therapeutic approach recognizes that healing must encompass both the emotional and the physical dimensions of our being.

Through guided movement and mindful awareness, the person learns to decipher the messages their body carries—messages that might have been silenced by words alone.

As the person moves through various postures and gestures, they begin to access reservoirs of emotional insight that were previously dormant.

By embracing movement and awareness as tools of healing, this approach invites us to explore the stories held within our physical sensations.

Let's remember that therapy isn't just about addressing symptoms; it's about fostering transformation. Attachment-informed therapies offer a way to rewrite old scripts, heal relational wounds, and step into a future guided by secure connections. These therapies become bridges from pain to healing, from uncertainty to growth. Through the interplay of attachment insights and therapeutic practices, individuals discover the power within them to mend what's broken, nurture what's vital, and embrace the journey towards emotional well-being.

NOTES

NOTES

NOTES

NOTES

10

Nurturing Attachment in Adoptive and Foster Families

Think about the journey of children adopted from orphanages or foster care. For them, the road to attachment can be rocky, marked by the echoes of early disruptions, neglect, and trauma. These young hearts carry the weight of experiences that challenge secure attachment. It's like navigating through a maze where trust feels distant, and bonds are fragile.

The Healing Power of Caregivers

Picture a world where caregivers are not just caretakers, but also healers. Therapeutic parenting approaches emerge as a guiding light, illuminating the path towards emotional restoration for children who have faced the storms of insecurity and neglect. These caregivers become the architects of healing, constructing a secure framework within which attachment wounds can be mended.

Imagine a child who has known the sting of abandonment or the weight of unmet needs. Now, picture them in the embrace of a therapeutic parent. These parents are like anchors, grounding the child amidst the waves of uncertainty. Their consistency and attunement become a safe haven, a sanctuary where the child's fears and vulnerabilities can find refuge.

Therapeutic parents are akin to skilled gardeners, tending to the delicate blossoms of attachment. They recognize that these blossoms might have been stunted or bruised by early experiences, and they approach their role with a nurturing touch. Just as a gardener tends to each plant's unique needs, therapeutic parents tailor their approach to suit the child's attachment style and history.

Envision a child's trust slowly taking root, nurtured by the presence of a caregiver who understands the importance of responsiveness. These caregivers through their actions, communicate a powerful message: "You are seen, you are heard, and you are valued."

Therapeutic parenting is a testament to the resilience of the human spirit. It acknowledges that attachment wounds can be healed, even when the scars run deep.

Therapeutic parenting is not a solitary journey, but a collective effort to mend what has been broken. Just as a village comes together to rebuild after a storm, caregivers, professionals, and support networks collaborate to mend attachment wounds. Through their collective dedication, they pave the way for children to rewrite their narratives and step into a future where secure bonds and emotional well-being take center stage.

Nurturing Trust through Treatment

Imagine stepping into a therapy room, a haven of healing where children and caregivers embark on a transformative journey. Within these walls, the echoes of attachment wounds begin to fade, replaced by the gentle hum of hope and resilience. This therapy room becomes a sanctuary, a space where the tangled threads of attachment can be carefully unraveled and rewoven.

Here, the focus is on more than just addressing surface-level behaviors; it's about delving deep into the heart of the trauma triggers that have left their imprints on the tapestry of attachment. It's like exploring the layers of a complex puzzle, seeking to understand the intricate connections between past experiences and present reactions.

Therapeutic treatment is akin to learning a new language, one that equips caregivers with the tools to respond compassionately and effectively to the challenges that arise. Just as learning a language opens doors to new cultures and experiences, this therapeutic journey opens doors to healthier ways of connecting and nurturing attachment bonds.

Imagine a caregiver facing the storms of a child's rages and avoidance. Instead of responding with frustration or helplessness, they draw from the lessons learned in therapy. They navigate these tempestuous waters with newfound understanding, offering a lifeline of safety and support to the child. The therapy room becomes a training ground for resilience, where caregivers learn to weather the storms while keeping the flame of trust alive.

In the therapy room, attachment wounds become not just scars, but opportunities for transformation. The walls bear witness to the tears shed, the struggles faced, and the victories celebrated. Through the dedication of caregivers, the expertise of therapists, and the power of therapeutic treatment, a child's story evolves from one of pain to one of triumph—a story where attachment wounds are mended and trust is nurtured, one session at a time.

The Supportive Web of Community

Support groups are a web of understanding and empathy. These groups are like gatherings around a campfire, where adoptive and foster parents share stories, insights, and challenges. In this space, struggles are met with understanding, and triumphs are celebrated together. It's a community where attachment challenges are understood, and the journey towards secure bonds is walked hand in hand.

The Promise of Earned Security

Hold on to the promise of earned security. It's a promise that speaks of transformation, of children finding the roots of trust in the embrace of new caregivers. It's a promise that caregivers can rewrite the stories of attachment, one nurturing moment at a time. In the world of adoptive and foster families, attachment isn't just a challenge; it's a journey of hope. Through therapeutic approaches, unwavering care, and the support of a community, attachment blooms anew, offering children a chance to rewrite their stories and caregivers a chance to be the authors of healing and growth.

NOTES

NOTES

NOTES

NOTES

11

Nurturing Healthy Relationships:

This chapter is as a toolkit, filled with skills that enrich bonds, strengthen connections, and elevate our ability to relate with authenticity and depth. In this journey, we explore the art of developing secure relating skills that breathe life into close connections.

Cultivating Emotional Intelligence

Imagine emotional intelligence as a universal language of the heart, a language that allows us to communicate not just with others, but with ourselves on a deeper level. Just as we learn to speak our native tongue, we can also embark on a journey to understand and navigate the intricate world of emotions. This journey is akin to exploring an expansive landscape, where each emotion is a vibrant hue waiting to be discovered.

Increasing self-awareness is like peering into a treasure chest of emotions, each one waiting to be unearthed and examined. Just as an artist discovers the various colors on their palette, we begin to uncover the shades and nuances of our emotional experiences. This heightened self-awareness is like being handed a key that unlocks the door to a richer, more nuanced understanding of ourselves.

As we delve deeper into this emotional landscape, we begin to label our feelings with greater precision. It's like finding the perfect word to capture the essence of an emotion, transforming it from an abstract sensation to a concrete expression. Just as a painter selects the perfect color to convey a specific mood, we choose words that accurately represent the emotions swirling within us.

But emotional intelligence goes beyond just labeling emotions; it also involves perspective-taking. Picture standing on the shores of a vast ocean, gazing out at the horizon. Perspective-taking is like sailing across those waters, exploring emotions from various angles and viewpoints. It's about understanding that emotions are complex, influenced by our experiences, beliefs, and the world around us. Just as shifting our perspective changes how we perceive the vastness of the ocean, perspective-taking allows us to navigate the depths of our emotional experiences with empathy and insight.

As we develop our emotional intelligence, we begin to speak the language of the heart fluently. We become adept at deciphering our own emotional landscape and connecting with the emotions of others. This newfound language enhances our relationships, allowing us to communicate our feelings with clarity and empathy. It's like holding a key that opens doors to deeper connections, fostering a sense of understanding and intimacy.

Imagine having a conversation with someone in this language of emotions. It's like sharing a secret code that transcends words, a code that conveys not just the surface-level content of our interactions, but the underlying emotions that shape our experiences. Emotional intelligence becomes the bridge that connects us, allowing us to navigate the complex terrain of human emotions with grace and authenticity.

Crafting the Art of Communication

Imagine communication as a beautifully constructed bridge that spans the distance between two hearts. This bridge is crafted with care, built upon the pillars of assertive expression, empathic listening, and the delicate art of compromise. Just as an architect designs a bridge to withstand the elements, we design our communication to withstand the challenges of human interaction.

At the foundation of this bridge is assertive expression. It's like laying the strong stones that support the weight of our thoughts, feelings, and needs. Assertive expression allows us to speak our truth with clarity and confidence, without diminishing our own voice or overpowering others. It's about finding the words that accurately convey our thoughts, even if they're vulnerable or uncomfortable.

As we step onto this bridge, we encounter empathic listening, a key that unlocks the door to deep understanding. Imagine empathic listening as a pair of open ears and an open heart. It's not just about hearing words; it's about being fully present to another person's words and emotions. Just as a skilled musician listens to the nuances of each note, we listen to the nuances of what's being shared, acknowledging not just the content, but the emotions and experiences behind the words.

Now, as we walk along this bridge, we reach the center, a space where compromise blooms. Compromise is like a well-tended garden where two parties come together, each offering something valuable to create a harmonious whole. Just as two rivers merge to form a single stream, compromise allows us to find middle ground, balancing our own needs with the needs of others. It's the art of finding a solution that benefits both parties, fostering harmony in relationships.

As we continue to cross this bridge of communication, we realize that it's not just a one-time construction; it's an ongoing process. Communication, like any skill, requires practice, patience, and a willingness to learn. It's about refining our ability to express ourselves assertively, listen empathically, and find compromises that strengthen connections.

Self-Awareness: The Compass Within

Self-awareness is like a reliable compass that you carry within yourself, ready to guide you through the intricate labyrinth of relationships. Just as explorers depend on a compass to find their way through uncharted territory, self-awareness becomes your guiding tool to navigate the complex landscape of human connections.

At the heart of this compass lies your attachment style, a map that provides insights into your patterns of behavior, emotions, and responses in relationships. This attachment style is like the key to deciphering the cryptic codes of your interactions. Just as a map shows you the landmarks and routes, your attachment style shows you the familiar patterns and tendencies that shape your relationships.

As you gaze upon this map of your attachment style, you begin to recognize the threads that have been woven into the fabric of your interactions. These threads represent the experiences and relationships that have influenced your approach to connection and intimacy. It's like holding a mirror to your history, seeing the reflections of past experiences that have shaped who you are today.

But this compass doesn't stop at showing you the terrain; it also helps you identify the potential obstacles along the way. Imagine being able to spot triggers and tendencies that might lead to emotional turbulence. These triggers are like warning signs on the road, guiding you to proceed with caution. With this awareness, you can navigate challenging situations with greater understanding and foresight.

And just as a skilled explorer discovers hidden treasures on their journey, self-awareness unveils the treasures of insight and understanding. By identifying your attachment style, triggers, and tendencies, you uncover the hidden gems of self-knowledge. These gems empower you to make informed choices, respond thoughtfully, and cultivate healthier patterns in your relationships.

As you use this compass of self-awareness, you gain a profound advantage in your journey through relationships. You become attuned to the contours of your emotional landscape, recognizing the twists and turns that lead to deeper connection or potential pitfalls. With each step guided by self-awareness, you find yourself navigating with wisdom and grace, moving closer to the destination of thriving relationships.

The Sanctuary of Mindfulness

Mindfulness is a sanctuary, a space where we can stand still amidst the chaos of emotions. It's like a calm oasis in the desert of our thoughts. Mindfulness involves staying anchored in the present, rather than getting swept away by the tide of difficult emotions. It's a tool that empowers us to respond, not react, to the challenges life throws our way.

The Symphony of Self-Regulation

Self-regulation is a symphony, where emotions and rational thinking dance in harmony. It's like a conductor guiding the orchestra of our reactions. Self-regulation involves managing emotional reactions, quelling anxiety and avoidance, and thinking rationally even under stress. It's the art of maintaining our emotional equilibrium in the face of life's storms.

The Dance of Mutuality

Now, picture mutuality as a dance, a graceful interplay of power and vulnerability. Mutuality involves sharing the stage, allowing both partners in a relationship to have a voice. It's being vulnerable, revealing our authentic selves, and responding to vulnerability with empathy. Mutuality is a duet where partners take turns leading and following, creating a harmonious rhythm of connection.

Secure relating isn't a destination; it's a lifelong journey. These skills are the threads we weave into the tapestry of our connections, creating bonds that are resilient, nurturing, and authentic. In the realm of healthy relating, we become artists, painting our relationships with the hues of emotional intelligence, the strokes of effective communication, and the canvas of mutual respect. Through these skills, we find that the journey itself is a destination of growth, intimacy, and fulfillment.

NOTES

NOTES

NOTES

NOTES

NOTES

NOTES

12

Stories of Transformation

Next we step into the shoes of those whose stories illuminate the path towards attachment transformation. These are real live stories shared by those who have had professional therapeutic support.

Navigating the Depths of Abandonment Fears

The story of Bill : his heart a labyrinth of anxieties and jealousy. His story is like a mirror reflecting the shadows of core abandonment fears. Through the lens of attachment, he embarks on a journey of self-discovery. It's like unearthing buried treasures within, unlocking the doors to healing. His journey is one of courage, as he learns to navigate the depths of his emotions, managing his jealousy through newfound understanding.

Bill's tale encapsulates the transformative power of attachment theory. As he begins to recognize the roots of his anxieties and the connection they have to his early attachment experiences, a profound shift occurs. Through introspection and self-awareness, he unveils the links between his past and present emotional responses. His journey is not just about understanding his jealousy, but also about embracing vulnerability and seeking growth.

With the guidance of a therapist versed in attachment theory, he learns to decode the messages his emotions carry. He grasps that his intense jealousy isn't merely a reflection of his partner's actions, but a projection of his deep-seated fears of being abandoned and unworthy of love. This revelation paves the way for him to reframe his perceptions, challenge his assumptions, and communicate more openly with his partner.

Through their therapeutic journey, Bill and his partner embark on a shared exploration of attachment dynamics. They learn to create a safe space for vulnerability, empathy, and compassion. As he gains insight into his attachment style and its impact on his relationship patterns, he becomes empowered to reshape his responses. With each step forward, he chips away at the walls he once erected in self-defense, gradually replacing them with bridges of connection.

His journey is not without its challenges. Progress is measured in moments of self-regulation, where he chooses to respond thoughtfully instead of reacting impulsively. He confronts his fears head-on, engages in constructive conversations with his partner, and nurtures a sense of security that he had once thought unattainable.

The transformation is gradual, but significant. Bill's commitment to navigating the depths of his abandonment fears leads to a profound shift in his relationship dynamics. He learns to replace jealousy with trust, anxiety with emotional attunement, and insecurity with a growing sense of self-worth.

His story is a testament to the potential of attachment theory to guide individuals toward healthier, more secure bonds. Through introspection, vulnerability, and the willingness to rewrite the narratives of their past, individuals like him can transform their lives and relationships. It's a journey that requires courage, patience, and a deep desire for growth. A journey that ultimately leads to the invaluable reward of authentic and secure connections.

Parenthood: A Voyage of Healing

The story of Antoinette, her heart a canvas of unhealed wounds. Her journey into parenthood becomes a vessel of transformation. It's like tending to a garden, nurturing the seeds of earned security. As she cradles her child, she also cradles her own past, offering a chance for wounds inflicted by an unaffectionate father to find closure. Her journey is one of resilience, as she learns to rewrite the script of her past through the bonds of motherhood.

In the embrace of motherhood, she discovers a profound opportunity for healing. As she gazes into her child's eyes, she's confronted with the reflections of her own childhood. The memories of her unaffectionate father resurface, intertwined with her newfound role as a mother. It's as if she holds the power to mend the fractures of her past while nurturing the growth of a secure attachment with her child.

Attachment theory serves as her compass, guiding her through uncharted territories of emotions and memories. With each cuddle and soothing lullaby, she begins to unravel the threads of her own attachment experiences. It's a process of unwrapping, layer by layer, the narratives that have shaped her sense of self and her expectations of love.

With the support of a therapist who understands the intricate interplay of attachment and healing, she embarks on a journey of exploration. She learns to decipher the echoes of her past in her present reactions, finding connections between her own attachment style and the emotional landscape of her parenting journey. This newfound awareness fuels her determination to nurture a secure bond with her child, to provide the warmth and affection she yearned for as a child.

As the days turn into months, her relationship with her child becomes a canvas for rewriting her history. She finds solace in creating an environment of emotional safety and attunement. Through her commitment to learning and growth, she learns to decipher her child's cues, respond sensitively, and provide the nurturing presence she wished for in her own early years.

The voyage of healing isn't without its challenges. She grapples with moments of self-doubt and the echoes of her father's emotional absence. But with each hurdle she faces head-on, she gains strength and resilience. She dismantles the barriers that once held her back and embraces vulnerability as a source of empowerment.

As her child's laughter fills the air and the tender moments of connection multiply, she realizes the transformative power of parenthood. Through her journey of nurturing and healing, she uncovers the potential to rewrite her narrative and forge a new path. She's no longer defined solely by her wounds; she's also a vessel of love, growth, and the promise of secure attachment.

Her story is a testament to the healing potential embedded in the journey of parenthood. With attachment theory as her guide, she navigates the currents of her emotions, cultivating a legacy of emotional security for her child and herself. It's a voyage that transcends generations, rewriting the script of her past while sowing the seeds of a more connected and nurturing future.

Reconnecting Through Vulnerability

The story of Mark and Greta, their relationship a tapestry of fractures and reconnections. Their journey involves peeling back the layers of past traumas, like uncovering ancient ruins of emotions. Attachment theory becomes their guide, as they learn to reveal and heal past wounds. It's like rebuilding a bridge that had once crumbled. Through vulnerability, they mend what's broken and embrace the intimacy they had longed for.

Their journey of reconnection begins with a shared understanding that their relationship is a reflection of their individual attachment histories. As they embark on this voyage, they realize that their interactions hold the key to their healing. Every argument, every moment of closeness, carries echoes of their attachment styles, revealing patterns that have been etched into the fabric of their relationship.

With the guidance of a skilled therapist who navigates the waters of attachment dynamics, they dive deep into their emotional landscapes. Through open conversations, they expose the vulnerabilities that have remained hidden for far too long. Greta, haunted by a history of anxious attachment, confronts her fears of abandonment that have fueled her insecurities. Mark, bearing the weight of avoidant attachment, uncovers the layers of emotional distance he had erected as a defense mechanism.

Their journey becomes a process of mutual revelation, as they share their stories of past hurts and longings. In the safe container of therapy, they learn to decode each other's emotional signals, recognizing the cries for closeness beneath the surface conflicts. Attachment theory offers them a framework to decipher the unspoken language of their emotions, fostering a newfound empathy for each other's experiences.

As they navigate the terrain of their relationship, they find opportunities for healing in the most unexpected moments. A shared laugh becomes a bridge across the chasm of their insecurities. A gentle touch serves as a reminder that they are not alone in their journey. Through each vulnerable confession, they rewrite the narrative of their connection, transforming moments of tension into catalysts for growth.

With every step forward, their bond strengthens. Mark's tendency to withdraw is met with the Greta's reassurance, providing the security he needs to open up. Her anxieties are met with his patience and understanding, soothing the echoes of her past wounds. Through their shared vulnerability, they build a foundation of trust, rewriting the script of their relationship from one of discord to one of emotional safety.

Their journey is not without its challenges. Moments of resistance and regression remind them of the depths of their attachment patterns. Yet, armed with newfound insights, they confront these challenges head-on. They lean into vulnerability, using it as a bridge to cross the divides that once seemed insurmountable.

As they continue on this path of reconnection, they marvel at the transformation that has taken place. Their relationship, once defined by fractures, has been woven back together with threads of authenticity and understanding. Attachment theory has provided them with a roadmap to navigate their journey, but it's their shared vulnerability that has illuminated the path to healing. In each moment of openness, they mend what's broken, rekindling the intimacy they had always longed for.

The Dance of Disorganized Attachment

The story of Samantha: an individual with disorganized attachment, their emotions a tempest of chaos. Their journey is like a dance, a gradual rhythm of resolution. Therapeutic relating becomes their partner, offering stability amidst the storm. Attachment theory becomes their choreographer, guiding their steps towards emotional balance. Through persistence and guidance, their dance transforms from chaos to coherence.

At the beginning of their journey, Samantha's emotional landscape is a maze of contradictions. They yearn for closeness, yet fear it. They seek comfort, yet shy away from it. This dance of disorganized attachment is a struggle between the desire for safety and the haunting echoes of past traumas.

Therapeutic intervention becomes their anchor. With a skilled therapist as their guide, they begin to unravel the knots of their emotions. The therapist becomes a steady presence in their life, a source of reliability in a sea of uncertainty. Through patient exploration, they dive into the depths of their attachment history, unearthing the roots of their disorganized dance.

As they share their stories, a pattern emerges. The chaos of their emotional reactions is traced back to moments of unpredictability in their past. Neglect, trauma, or inconsistent caregiving have left scars that continue to shape their present. With attachment theory as their compass, they decode the hidden messages of their behaviors, understanding that their dance is a desperate attempt to navigate the unpredictability they once faced.

In each session, they take steps towards vulnerability, revealing the layers of their disorganized attachment. The therapist responds with attunement and empathy, offering a secure base from which to explore their emotions. This new dance partner becomes a mirror, reflecting back their experiences and providing a fresh perspective.

With time and practice, the individual learns to recognize their triggers and responses, gaining insight into the origins of their emotional storms. Attachment theory offers them a language to articulate their experiences, helping them make sense of the intricate steps they've been taking.

They practice leaning into discomfort, allowing themselves to experience vulnerability without spiraling into chaos. The therapist's steady presence becomes an anchor, a safe haven where they can explore their emotions without fear of judgment. The journey is not without setbacks. Old patterns may resurface, and the familiar chaos may threaten to take over. But armed with the tools they've gained, they are better equipped to navigate these challenges. Attachment theory has given them a roadmap to understand their dance, and the therapeutic relationship has provided them with a safe space to practice new steps.

With each session, they rewrite the choreography of their emotions, shifting from chaos to clarity. Through their persistence and the guidance of attachment theory, they find a sense of equilibrium embodying the journey from chaos to coherence.

Stories of Inspiration and Hope

Remember that attachment patterns are not just concepts in textbooks; they are the threads that weave through the tapestry of real lives. Through these stories, we find inspiration and hope. We learn that our histories need not define us, that the pages of our past can be rewritten through the actions of the present. These stories are a testament to the power of human resilience, the strength of the human spirit, and the transformative journey towards secure attachment. Just as these individuals have navigated their paths, so too can we navigate our own, stepping into a future where relationships are nurtured, bonds are strengthened, and the narrative of attachment transformation continues to unfold.

NOTES

NOTES

NOTES

NOTES

NOTES

13

Embracing Attachment's Legacy and Forging Ahead

This book is a tapestry woven with threads of attachment theory - a vibrant mosaic that reveals the intricate dance of human bonds. We've explored the foundations, research, interventions, and applications that make up this captivating framework. Attachment theory isn't just a concept; it's a lens that transforms how we perceive relationships and human development.

Illuminating the Impact of Early Bonds

Attachment theory is as a lantern, shedding light on the pathways of human growth. We've delved into its power to illuminate the impact of early bonding on our development. Just as light dispels darkness, attachment theory has shone a light on the intricate patterns that shape our lives, offering insights that transcend disciplines from psychology to social work, from education to clinical practice.

A Lens for Self-Understanding and Growth

Attachment theory is a mirror that reflects the intricate contours of our inner world. Through this lens, we've discovered that our attachment patterns are not fixed destinies. They're malleable landscapes waiting to be explored. Attachment theory becomes a compass, guiding us towards self-understanding and growth. It's a compass that helps us chart our course towards healthier bonds and resilient connections.

Exploring New Frontiers

Envision the future as a canvas yet to be painted, where attachment theory's influence continues to expand. We stand at the threshold of new frontiers, with longitudinal studies and neurobiological research as our guiding stars. Cultural variations await our exploration, revealing the tapestry of attachment across diverse landscapes. Innovative interventions hold the promise of transformation, reaching those who seek the embrace of secure bonds.

The Promise of Flourishing Attachments

The legacy of attachment theory lives on in each of us. The insights we've gained are the seeds of a more interconnected and compassionate world. The promise of secure attachments isn't just a theoretical concept; it's a tangible reality that unfolds as we embark on our own journeys of growth and transformation.

So, let us step forward with hope and determination. Let us continue to unravel the mysteries of attachment, explore the depths of our relationships, and cultivate bonds that enrich our lives. The tapestry of attachment theory has brought us to this moment, and the story it tells is one of resilience, connection, and the enduring journey towards the heart of what it means to be human.

REFERENCES

Ainsworth, M.D.S. (1979). Infant–mother attachment. American Psychologist, 34, 932-937.

Ainsworth, M. D. S., Blehar, M. C., Waters, E., & Wall, S. (1978). Patterns of attachment: A psychological study of the strange situation. Hillsdale, NJ: Erlbaum.

Bowlby, J. (1969). Attachment and loss: Vol. 1. Attachment. New York: Basic Books.

Bowlby, J. (1988). A secure base: Parent-child attachment and healthy human development. New York: Basic Books.

Bretherton, I. (1992). The origins of attachment theory: John Bowlby and Mary Ainsworth. Developmental psychology, 28, 759-775.

Cassidy, J., & Shaver, P.R. (Eds.). (2008). Handbook of attachment: Theory, research and clinical applications. New York, NY: Guilford Press.

Fraley, R.C., Roisman, G.I., & Haltigan, J.D. (2013). The legacy of early experiences in development: Formalizing alternative models of how early experiences are carried forward over time. Developmental psychology, 49(1), 109-126.

Main, M., Hesse, E., & Hesse, S. (2011). Attachment theory and research: Overview with suggested applications to child custody. Family Court Review, 49(3), 426-463.

Siegel, D.J. (2001). Toward an interpersonal neurobiology of the developing mind: Attachment relationships, "mindsight," and neural integration. Infant Mental Health Journal, 22(1-2), 67-94.

Sroufe, L.A., Egeland, B., Carlson, E.A., & Collins, W.A. (2005). The development of the person: The Minnesota Study of Risk and Adaptation from Birth to Adulthood. New York, NY: Guilford Press.

APPENDIX: Resources for Further Learning

Explore the wealth of knowledge on attachment theory and its applications through these recommended resources:

Websites:

- Psychology Today on Attachment: Delve into articles and insights on attachment theory's intricacies and impact. Visit: https://www.psychologytoday.com/us/basics/attachment

- Circle of Security International: Discover practical tools and programs for fostering secure attachments. Explore: https://www.circleofsecurityinternational.com

- Attachment Network: Engage with a community focused on attachment-related discussions and resources. Access: http://attachmentnetwork.org/

Books:

- Attached by Levine and Heller: Uncover how attachment styles influence romantic relationships and learn strategies for building stronger bonds.

- Hold Me Tight by Sue Johnson: Dive into the world of emotionally focused therapy and how it can transform relationships.

- The Body Keeps the Score by Bessel van der Kolk: Explore the profound connection between trauma, attachment, and the body's responses.

Online Courses:

- DIY attachment theory Workshop with JulieAnn Poole: Take charge of your learning journey with this interactive online workshop exploring attachment theory's nuances.

- Making Sense of Your Life with Dr. Dan Siegel: Delve into the intersections of neuroscience, psychology, and attachment in this enlightening course.

Podcasts:

- Relationships Made Simple: Tune in to practical insights and advice for navigating relationships through an attachment lens.

- The attachment theory Podcast: Deepen your understanding of attachment theory's real-world applications through engaging discussions.

Support Communities:

- ATAA (Association for Treatment and Attachment in Adoption): Connect with a community dedicated to fostering secure attachments in adopted children and their families.

- Attachment & Trauma Treatment Centre for Healing Facebook Group: Join a supportive online space focused on healing attachment-related wounds and promoting growth.

www.ingramcontent.com/pod-product-compliance
Ingram Content Group UK Ltd.
Pitfield, Milton Keynes, MK11 3LW, UK
UKHW020652041125
8754UKWH00037B/717

9 781738 458608